THE END
OF THE
ZODIAC
MYSTERY

THE END
OF THE
ZODIAC
MYSTERY

HOW FORENSIC SCIENCE HELPED SOLVE ONE OF THE
MOST INFAMOUS SERIAL KILLER CASES OF THE CENTURY

MICHAEL N. WAKSHULL
CQE, MSc

Book Design by Genius Book Services
Cover by Cyrus Wraith Walker and Steven W. Booth
Interior by Steven W. Booth
    www.GeniusBookServices.com

ISBN: 978-0-9857294-2-4

Library of Congress Control Number: 2014909134

Quality 9 Consulting, Inc.
PO Box 892965
Temecula, CA 92589

Table of Contents

Acknowledgments

This book is dedicated to people without whom
I could not have presented the work

- My wife, Jan Tucker, is the best editor I know. She worked tirelessly to make the content of the book flow, add more human interest, and make sure it would be understandable to readers who might be unfamiliar with document examination. She also ensured proper grammar and sentence structure. Although she was disturbed by the subject matter of the case, I thank her for fully supporting my efforts to work on it.

- Susan Mustafa and Gary L. Stewart for placing their faith in my ability to perform the work and their willingness to accept the results, whatever they would be.

- Thank you to all my Document Examination and Quality teachers who selflessly shared their knowledge.

Introduction

This is the story of traces left by a father, discovered 40 years later by the son he had cruelly abandoned and never knew. These traces told the son more than he ever wanted to know about his father.

This book explains how I came to assist authors Gary L. Stewart and Susan Mustafa by adding a final layer of certainty in their search for the true identity of Gary's father, Earl Van Best Jr. The book, *The Most Dangerous Animal of All* by Gary L. Stewart with Susan Mustafa, tells the chilling story of how Gary came to learn who his father really was.

Forensic document examination, which includes analyzing and comparing handwriting, among other specialties, is widely used to identify altered documents. In this case, I used forensic handwriting examination to help shed light on the real identity of Gary's father.

We always leave traces of ourselves wherever we go. These traces contain evidence that may eventually be discovered. In 1962, Earl Van Best Jr. wrote some information on a marriage certificate. Fifty years later this marriage certificate would be associated with the writings of a serial killer who had never been caught—until now.

By reading this book, you will gain an insider perspective of how I worked this intriguing forensic case.

You will walk step-by-step through the logic I used and the comparisons I discovered in the handwriting of this vicious killer. The information provided is not intended to substitute for the detailed report I delivered to Susan approximately two months after first speaking with her about the case. You can find that report in the Appendix.

The report is a thorough description of my research findings, and it includes copies of actual documents written by the man who called himself the Zodiac killer. I used these documents to identify him using the scientific procedures described here.

As you read this book and the report that follows, you will learn how forensic handwriting examination—the final piece of evidence in the case—was used to put an end to this macabre mystery.

Having conducted scientific research in the discipline of handwriting identification, this case presented an interesting challenge. I have been an invited speaker at international forensic conferences including the World Congress of Forensics in China, have authored legal continuing education classes in document examination and other works, and I work on criminal as well as civil cases.

Regardless of the results of the examination, I knew this would be an interesting case to cite. A document examiner colleague had worked on the case of Jack the Ripper in London, which resulted in eliminating the suspect as being the killer. The people who retained him had been certain the suspect was the killer.

How the Investigation Began

On a hot summer day in August 2012, my wife, Jan, said, "One of these days you're going to get a famous case." It turned out she was prophetic.

Two months later, while listening attentively to a speaker at a document examiners' conference in Phoenix, my cell phone vibrated. The call was from an area code I didn't recognize.

Reluctantly, I left the conference room to answer the phone. Perhaps this would be a new client. Usually when I miss a call, the person on the other end moves on to the next document examiner on the list without leaving a message. I didn't want to lose the prospective business.

The caller said, "I'm Susan Mustafa, and I'm a true crime writer." She piqued my interest from the start. "I am researching a cold case where my co-author had been following traces left behind by his father—a father he never knew. The trail led him to believe his father was a famous serial killer." Suddenly this became even more interesting. Susan continued, "The more he tried to disprove this hypothesis, the stronger the evidence supported it."

Her co-author, Gary L. Stewart, had kept a detailed journal—now 500 pages in length—of all his research. He engaged Susan to help him turn the journal into a book. When she called me, she was at the critical point where she needed a document examiner to compare the serial killer's handwriting with Gary's father's handwriting from a marriage certificate his father had executed 50 years earlier in 1962.

This was not my typical client.

Susan clarified, "This involves the potential identification of the Zodiac Killer from the 1960s and 1970s in California." I was floored. Although I lived in New York at the time the Zodiac was terrorizing California residents, I remembered having been distressed by the fear aroused by news reports of the Zodiac killings so far away. The Son of Sam was closer to home in New York City. There were questions whether the two killers were the same person until David Berkowitz (Son of Sam) was caught.

Susan had already spoken with two other document examiners by the time she called me. She explained that the first had declined the opportunity saying the case was "just too creepy." The second said there simply was not enough evidence to work the case.

Being somewhat familiar with the Zodiac case, I knew that other document examiners and investigators had allegedly solved the cold case previously. Books had been written and movies made about how the case was solved. But each of the solutions had later proved to be mistaken.

A significant part of me wondered whether this was just another hopeful investigation with flawed data. I'd already been involved in many attorney cases where the results did not support the client's statement as to the authenticity of the writing.

The more adventuresome part of me was hopeful—I was ready for some additional interesting and challenging work. Although I was skeptical, Susan's information had aroused sufficient interest for me to look at the material. I was eager to determine whether there was enough data to conduct an investigation.

Susan needed someone who could think like a detective—not simply an analyst—and my training in science and engineering had taught me to think like a detective. Science is about trial and error. A scientific approach establishes a hypothesis. The focus of the examination is to refute the hypothesis.

The scientist—in this case the document examiner—tries to prove the hypothesis wrong rather than trying to prove it right. Proving it right increases the chance of falling into a confirmation bias, where supporting evidence is subconsciously given more weight than contradicting evidence.

If one approach to the hypothesis fails to yield a result, the scientist must try another approach until a result is reached. The final result might be inconclusive due to a lack of data or for other reasons. If the hypothesis cannot be refuted, the scientist accepts the hypothesis.

The Evidence

The self-named Zodiac killer, after revealing this sinister moniker, frequently taunted the police with notes, letters, and elaborate cryptograms—coded messages that he referred to as ciphers. *The Most Dangerous Animal of All* presents two cryptograms which allegedly contain his real name.

Prior to naming himself the Zodiac, he had already sent notes and letters to newspapers in the San Francisco Bay area and Riverside, California.

An early Zodiac killing, attributed to him years later, occurred in Riverside. The murderer, unknown at the time, had sent letters to the Riverside police, *The Riverside Press-Enterprise* newspaper, and the father of the murdered young lady. I currently live near Riverside—this case was of local interest to me.

Susan explained that copies of the letters, notes and envelopes sent by the Zodiac killer to various publications, people, and law enforcement agencies were available on a variety of websites.

Sufficiently convinced that there could be something to work with, I decided to move forward, and signed a nondisclosure agreement presented by Susan, forbidding me from revealing any information to anyone other than her until the date of book publication.

Susan sent me copies of the Zodiac letters. I also downloaded and printed copies of the Zodiac letters and other documents from the Internet. I began my investigation with enthusiasm.

At the same time, Susan emailed me a copy of the marriage certificate between Judith Chandler (Gary's mother) and Earl Van Best Jr., the suspected Zodiac killer. She told me Gary's father typically used the name Van Best since Earl was his father's name. The marriage certificate included his full name.

The quality of the image of the marriage certificate Susan emailed was not sufficient for examination, but she was able to send me a copy of the marriage certificate obtained from the Washoe County Clerk's office in Reno, Nevada by U.S. mail.

Susan also relayed there was substantial additional evidence linking Van to the Zodiac murders. This was territory I did not want to enter. It offered the potential to induce unwanted contextual bias. The less I knew about the circumstances of the case, the better.

An objective analysis requires as much blindness to the case as possible. Ideally, the investigator should perform the work without knowing the desired outcome of the requesting party and other background information surrounding the circumstances of the case.

A document examiner deals with handwriting and documents—all I really needed to see and consider were the available handwriting samples. Certain information such as injuries, illness, writing position, and other afflictions that can affect handwriting are valuable information for the examiner. In this case, none of this information about the writer of the Zodiac letters was available.

In real life, background information and the desired results typically are provided to independent examiners. We then must divorce ourselves from the context of each case and examine the evidence without concern for the requestor's desired outcome. The document examiner then reports the outcome presented by the evidence.

Van had been married three times. Susan sent two other marriage certificates to me and a jail booking sheet, all signed either Earl Van Best or Earl Van Best Jr. For the examination, I worked on the assumption these had been signed by Van.

The first marriage certificate was to Mary Annette Player, signed in 1957, five years before Van married Gary's mother, Judith. The second marriage was in 1966, to Edith Kos, four years after his marriage to Judith.

The only writing from Van on the first and the third marriage certificates was his signature. Regarding the second marriage certificate, Judith had attested to Gary that Van completed all the information except the witnesses' signatures, including her printed name.

Because I had only four documents for comparison, three of them containing only Van's signatures, my first impression was that the document examiner who had told Susan there was not enough information to perform a valid examination was correct.

Generally Accepted Practices in Handwriting Examination

Document examiners perform their work from a different perspective than most people realize. They do not set out to prove whether a document is authentic (unaltered) or not authentic or whether a document was or was not written by a specific person. They do not merely look at a document and immediately formulate an opinion of authenticity.

Using a scientific approach, document examiners carefully examine the intricacies of the available evidence—in this case handwriting. Handwriting examination involves comparing writing we know someone wrote, referred to as the known writing, against handwriting on documents where the writer has not been determined, called questioned writing.

An established practice in forensic document examination is that cursive writing and hand printing are generally not compared with each other. The character formations and the muscular interactions used to write each are different. The marriage certificate and the Zodiac's letters, except for the envelope to *The Press-Enterprise*, are hand printed.

An underlying concept in handwriting identification is that no person ever writes exactly the same way twice and no two people write exactly alike.

A good analogy is what happens when someone throws a ball. Each time they throw, the speed is slightly different. And the distance the ball travels also differs each time the ball is thrown.

Similarly, each time a person writes, the speed of the writing is different and the size of the writing is different. The spacing between letters and words is different. Sometimes this difference is so slight a person casually looking at the writing cannot notice the difference. These differences are known as variability in a person's handwriting.

The relative ratio of the height of the characters in each individual's writing (for example, how large the small letters are in proportion to the capital letters) remains relatively consistent in a person's writing. How the letters are shaped and slanted and where they fall in regard to the baseline, among other characteristics, also remain consistent. This is because writing is a habit.

A trained document examiner carefully measures the attributes of the writing and records this data to determine the qualitative and quantitative variability of the writing.

As a certified quality engineer with a degree in mathematics, I have studied the science of variability and I additionally apply this science when performing my examinations. I compared these proportions and slants for the writing both on Van's documents and the Zodiac letters.

Differences in the way characters are formed is a key aspect that helps identify a particular subject's handwriting. These formations are investigated at a micro level using a microscope or other means of magnification. The examiner looks for areas where a writer may consistently lift a pen, exert extra pressure in the writing, insert breaks between letters within words, and many other aspects that are unlikely to be replicated by someone other than the writer of the known document. In many cases, it would not be possible for someone other than the writer to replicate these distinct characteristics of the writing.

These micro-anomalies also account for variability in the writing. Many examples of a person's writing are required in order to determine how much the person varies their writing from session to session. Examples of known writing are called exemplars.

Since many people learn the same style of writing when they're young, it's not unusual to find similar attributes among the writing of different individuals. For this reason, a layperson may incorrectly determine that questioned writing was also written by the known writer, or conversely determine that the actual writer did not write a questioned document.

The trained document examiner looks beyond the overall structure of the writing and digs deeply into the details. He or she examines the known document(s) looking for unique characteristics consistently executed by a person.

When a preponderance of differences exists in the handwriting among documents, it may be determined that there is more than one writer. Alternately, finding one or two unique characteristics does not make a match of writers, since many people may exhibit the same characteristics in their writing. When a preponderance of unique characteristics appears in the known writing and these characteristics also appear in the questioned writing, a match may be declared.

The degree of certainty of the match depends on the degree of similarities and differences between the known and questioned writings. When there is a consistent difference between questioned writing and known exemplars, this often indicates different writers. For example, if a cursive upper case E appears consistently in the known writing but a block printed upper case E appears consistently in the questioned writing, this might indicate different writers. But even when many similarities and only a few differences exist, the differences may outweigh the similarities in reaching a conclusion about the authenticity of the writing.

Alternatively, when a consistent difference occurs, it may just be that the sample size of exemplars is too small. The document examiner might request additional exemplars to determine whether the difference persists. Occasionally I discover that something originally appearing as a difference becomes a known trait of the writer when I examine additional exemplars.

Common traits can occur when a person intentionally attempts to copy the writing of another person. An advantage I had in this investigation was that the writer of the Zodiac letters, if he was not Van, would not have known to imitate Van's writing. I could therefore treat the writings as being completely independent of each other.

So a document examiner draws an opinion based on the overall impression of the writing plus common anomalies found in both the questioned and the known writing.

Sufficiency of Evidence

In this case, I needed to consider whether the time span between Judith and Van's marriage certificate and the Zodiac letters presented a difficulty. The more contemporaneous the writing of the questioned document is to the known documents, the more reliable the document examiner's opinion. The marriage certificate was signed in January 1962. The Zodiac murders began in 1967 and continued until 1974.

Substantial research shows that once a person matures, their handwriting becomes a very difficult habit to break. Handwriting examiners often refer to handwriting as brain writing. This is because handwriting is a very complex, neuromuscular interaction where the brain sends signals to the muscles in the arm and hand, instructing which muscles need to contract in order to form the letters and words of writing.

Once people reach their early 20s, their writing style has been developed. In some instances, this habit develops at an earlier age. The writing style is based on how a person was taught to write, the desired look of their writing, and other personal inputs.

The developed writing style is often referred to in the industry as graphic maturity. Barring major illness, injury to the writing arm, a brain injury, or any other reason the handwriting may be adversely affected, the person's writing remains very similar over time after reaching graphic maturity.

Van was 27 years old when he married Judith and filled out his second marriage certificate. By this age, he would have established his writing habits and reached graphic maturity. These habits would have persisted for at least the next seven years, which includes the time of the Zodiac's writing. For this reason, I was comfortable comparing Van's handwriting in the marriage certificates and jail booking sheet with the Zodiac's writing.

Document examiners often request a minimum of 15 or more exemplars to determine the common attributes of the known writing. This is a typical starting point. The document examiner who told Susan not enough information was available to work on the case was considering the case from this perspective.

Although 60 samples had been allegedly generated by the Zodiac—providing a sufficient sample of questioned writing—the amount of known writing executed by Earl Van Best Jr. was insufficient.

After focusing on the problem, I realized I could take an alternative approach. This approach required a different way of looking at the case—actually working in reverse from the typical process while still following generally accepted practices of document examination.

Methodology Used to Compare the Alleged Zodiac Documents

The example writing comparisons included in the book, *The Most Dangerous Animal of All,* are a small subset of the total comparisons I made between the Zodiac's writing and the marriage certificate between Van and Judith, and other exemplars.

As you read through this methodology, you can follow along by finding copies of the Zodiac documents along with many more comparison exhibits in the report I prepared for Susan (included in the Appendix).

The first step I took for this case was to examine the letters, cards, envelopes, and other documents allegedly written by the Zodiac to determine whether or not all of them had been written by the same person.

Had they not been written by the same person, this would mean either the murders had been committed by multiple people or other people had been attempting to imitate the writer of the letters.

The reverse twist I developed for this case was this—I needed a sufficient amount of known writing. If I found that the alleged Zodiac documents had been written by one person, then I could treat those letters as the known writing.

To minimize potential bias, I formulated a hypothesis that the letters were written by different people. Would my investigation refute this hypothesis? Using this approach enabled me to proceed confidently with the examination.

I have a home office, and I first had to find a location in the house where I could lay out all the documents chronologically to get a good visual overview. The only reasonable place was the living room floor. My wife, Jan, said she didn't want this energy in our living room, yet she understood the importance of this case. For the three weeks they were there, she willed the documents out of her mind when entering the living room.

My analysis began.

Once I laid everything out, I was able to carefully examine all the documents to find common features in the different documents among the character formations and relationships.

To determine if the Zodiac documents had been written by different people, I read each of them looking for common words, characters, and character strings. I use the word characters to reference letters of the alphabet that are part of words. Character strings are multiple consecutive characters. Character formations are the way the letters are formed and placed on the page.

Comparing how the common characters were written would begin to provide evidence whether they had been written by different people.

Using the Adobe® Photoshop® software program (Photoshop), I extracted the common items from the Zodiac letters and placed each common character, character string or word on a separate Photoshop page for comparison purposes. I examined many examples of similar words and letters using this process. Three of these examples are shown in Figures 1 through 3.

Figure 1 compares the word *buttons* on four of the documents in question (the documents are labeled in red in the figure). You can see several similarities and some differences among the four samples, which I have indicated below the Figure. As you review these samples, keep in mind that the handwriting of all individuals is variable.

Dragon card 1970

Button cipher 1970

Kathleen Johns 1970

Little list page 1 1970

Figure 1 – Compare the Word *buttons*

Examples of similarities in Figure 1:

- The construction of the *b*
- The forward slant angle of the *b* in three of the samples
- The space between the *tt* and the following letter *o* in three of the samples
- The forward slant of the letters *tt*
- The formation of the letter *s*
- The placement and length of the cross stroke on the letters *t* in three of the samples
- The height proportion of the letters *b* and *t* relative to the other letters
- The height proportion of the letter *s* to the other letters

Examples of differences in Figure 1:

- In the Dragon card, the letters *tt* are completely separated. In the other samples, the cross bars on the *tt* touch each other.
- In the Dragon card the letters *ton* are run together. They are separate in the other examples.
- In the Little list sample, the writing is more vertical than in the other examples.
-

Figure 2 compares the word *bomb* from three documents. The lettering is virtually identical in each example. A slight difference is in the width of the letter *m* which is narrower in the Dragon card than in the Dear Melvin letter and Button cipher map.

The word bomb in the Dear Melvin letter is written slightly more vertically than in the Dragon card. In the Button cipher map the printing is right slanted. The overall structure of the character formations, the slant, inter-character spacing and other attributes are within the expected variability of the same writer's work.

Dragon card 1970

Dear Melvin 1969

Button cipher map 1970

Button cipher letter 1970

Figure 2 – Compare the Word *bomb*

Figure 3 shows the similarity in the character string *est* among six different documents. I selected *est* in order to compare the *est* in these documents with the *est* in Van's last name, Best, on the documents written by him.

The Lake Herman letters in this sample contained the 408 cipher described in *The Most Dangerous Animal of All*.

From *best* in
Exorcist letter
29-Jan-1974

From *west*
in Lake Herman
SF Examiner
31-Jul-1969

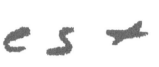

From *Western*
in Lake Herman
SF Examiner
31-Jul-1969

From *best*
in Citizen
8-May-1974

From *west*
in Lake Herman
Times-Herald
31-Jul-1969

Figure 3 – Compare the Character String *est*

Examples of similarities in Figure 3:
- There is substantially more space between the *st* than the *es*
- The relative height of the t-cross stroke on the stem relative to the height of the *s*
- The construction of the *s*
- The length of the t-cross
- The forward slant of the *est*

Examples of differences in Figure 3:
- The spacing between the characters in *west* in *The San Francisco Examiner* relative to the other characters
- The spacing difference is most prominent between the two Lake Herman letters written on July 31, 1969 to *The San Francisco Examiner*

Since the Lake Herman letters containing the 408 cipher were written on the same day, one would expect the writings to be very similar to each other. However, there are noticeable differences between the two. These differences show an expected variability in the Zodiac's writing style. Other writing that falls within this degree of variability indicates the same writer.

After I carefully examined all of the Zodiac documents, the result was an inability to show that the letters were written by different people, except for two instances. The last known Zodiac letter was written in 1974. Two letters written after this were not written by the person who wrote the other Zodiac letters. These are the 1978 letter written to KHJ-TV Channel 9 and the 1990 letter (see the Appendix).

These results led me to reject the hypothesis that the Zodiac documents were written by different people. I accepted the alternate hypothesis that the majority of the documents were written by the same person.

Methodology Used to Compare the Zodiac's and Earl Van Best Jr.'s Handwriting

In keeping with the reverse strategy I used for this case, which I began by determining that all but two of the alleged Zodiac documents were all written by the same person, I was able to treat these documents as the known writing.

My next step was to treat Van and Judith's marriage certificate and the other documents written by Van as questioned writing.

The question then became, "Is the marriage certificate written by the same person who wrote the Zodiac letters?" My new hypothesis was that the marriage certificate and the Zodiac letters were written by different people.

Comparison of Writing

Since I had fewer documents written by Van and many Zodiac documents, in order to reduce the complexity of this examination, I began to look for unique formations of characters and character strings on Van and Judith's marriage certificate.

If I could find the same unique formations in the Zodiac documents, I could then compare the documents for similarities and differences.

I found a sample of unique formations appearing in both sets of documents to work with and I marked them for comparison. Again I used Photoshop to extract the unique characters and words from the marriage certificate and the Zodiac letters. I made a comparison chart for each example and laid the characters out in matrix form (in columns and rows) in Photoshop.

Figure 4 compares the capital letter *J* between the marriage certificate and the Zodiac letters using side-by-side comparison. The top row shows two letter *J*s from the marriage certificate. The subsequent rows show *J*s from the Zodiac letters. The letters are displayed in colors for ease of differentiation.

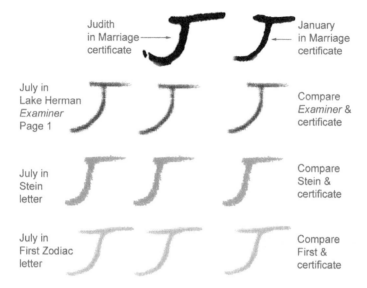

Figure 4 – Compare the Capital Letter *J* Using Side-by-Side Comparison

Comparison of the two letter *J*s in the marriage certificate demonstrates the variation that can occur in the same short document when a person writes the same character.

The *J*s in the left column are from the Zodiac letters labeled in red on the left. These *J*s were copied across the row for ease of comparing with the *J*s in the marriage certificate.

Figure 5 shows a much more accurate way of comparing the letters displayed in Figure 4. The naked eye is not the best tool to use when making these comparisons. Photoshop is far superior.

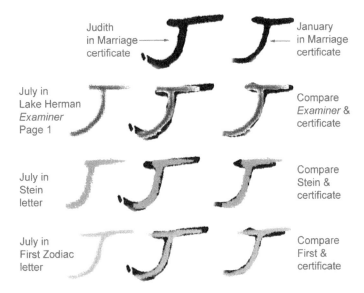

Figure 5 – Compare the Capital Letter _J_ Using Photoshop

Photoshop provides the capability to proportionally size an image—changing its size without changing its proportion. This same concept is used to enlarge or reduce a photograph while keeping the proportions constant.

In Figure 5, I used this technique to enlarge each character (letter _J_) to approximately the same height, automatically resizing the width proportionally. The dimensions of the entire character were changed at the same rate.

I then overlaid the colored characters from the Zodiac documents onto the black characters from the marriage certificate using Photoshop. This procedure permits a direct comparison of characters from multiple documents.

Given that there is variability in Mr. Best's writing in the same document (his marriage certificate with Judith), you would also expect variability among different documents also written by Mr. Best.

In keeping with the hypothesis, to see if the marriage certificate and the Zodiac documents were written by two different people, I needed to make a determination about the variability of the writing. To do this, I examined whether or not the characters from the marriage certificate were within the expected variability of the Zodiac's writing.

Figure 5 clearly shows that the formation and apparent construction of the letter *J* is virtually identical in the Zodiac letters and the marriage certificate. This indicates the writing was performed by the same person.

However, a single similarity can be a coincidence. This means I needed to perform the same exercise with as many common characters and character strings as possible.

Figure 6 shows the comparison of a common character string in the marriage certificate and different envelopes the Zodiac sent to the newspapers in San Francisco. The phrase *San Fran* was common to both.

The top row shows the two occurrences of *San Fran* in the marriage certificate. Van wrote both. The first entry was for Van's address. The second was for Judith's address. The name, San Francisco was written out. The Zodiac letters to the newspapers used only *San Fran*.

Each row shows the words *San Fran* as printed in the Zodiac document identified by the red label on the left. I overlaid the colored text from the marriage certificate on the black text from each Zodiac document.

Figure 6 – Compare the Phrase *San Fran*

I used the same Photoshop overlay technique to compare the phrase *San Fran* in Figure 6 that I had used to compare the letter *J* in Figure 5. The lines underneath the words in the Figure are directly from the marriage certificate.

My examination revealed that the construction of the letters, spacing, and other features were similar in all except one document. The envelope from 1990 showed a different character formation, spacing, and other attributes than the other examples of the Zodiac's writing and the marriage certificate.

Figure 7 shows the character string *est* from *Best* in the marriage certificate added to the Figure 3 comparison.

In this step, to determine if Mr. Best (the writer of the marriage certificate), was not also the writer of the Zodiac letters, I used the same type of comparison I had made in Figure 3.

I sized the characters proportionally to approximately the same size using the Photoshop method described above. Then I placed the colored Zodiac letters over the writing from the marriage certificate.

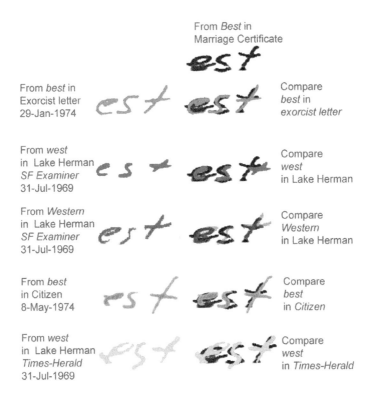

From *Best* in
Marriage Certificate

From *best* in
Exorcist letter
29-Jan-1974

Compare
best in
exorcist letter

From *west*
in Lake Herman
SF Examiner
31-Jul-1969

Compare
west
in Lake Herman

From *Western*
in Lake Herman
SF Examiner
31-Jul-1969

Compare
Western
in Lake Herman

From *best*
in Citizen
8-May-1974

Compare
best
in *Citizen*

From *west*
in Lake Herman
Times-Herald
31-Jul-1969

Compare
west
in *Times-Herald*

Figure 7 – Compare the Characters *est* from the Marriage Certificate with *est* from the Zodiac Letters

The comparison of the marriage certificate to the Zodiac letters shows many similarities and some differences. The question is whether the differences can be accounted for as variations in the Zodiac's writing.

Examples of similarities in Figure 7:

- The *es* characters are closer together than the *st* characters.
- The relative height of the t-cross on the stem is similar.
- The *s* is taller than the *e.*
- The forward slant of the *t* is similar.
- The construction of the letter *e* is the same.
- The structure of the *s* is the same in the marriage certificate and three of the Zodiac letters.

A difference in Figure 7:

- The Zodiac's writing is all right slanted. In the Marriage certificate the *es* is more vertical.

Comparing the Cursive Writing

The envelope addressed to *The Press-Enterprise* newspaper in Riverside had been executed in cursive style. This differed from the other Zodiac letters, which had been printed.

I thought about whether I could compare this writing with Earl Van Best Jr.'s signatures on the marriage certificates with Mary Player and Edith Kos and the jail booking sheet.

Typically document examiners compare signatures with signatures. But this comparison would compare signatures and regular handwriting. Also, this situation involved only a single document that had been written by the Zodiac.

It would be possible to compare the upper case *E* in *Earl* on Mr. Best's various documents with *E* in the word *Enterprise* on the Zodiac's envelope. *Enterprise* had not been completely spelled out on the envelope. It had also been crossed out with a line. See Exhibit 33 in the Appendix.

I looked to see if any other examples were available for comparison. I found that the Zodiac's letter to Mr. Bates had a printed *E* in the word *MORE* (Exhibit 11). But the printed *E* was a Greek-style *E*, just like the cursive writing in Mr. Best's signatures and the Zodiac's letter to *The Press-Enterprise*. This *E* also had a line through it.

I decided it was worth a try just to see the outcome. I used Photoshop's eraser tool to delete the lines through the writing, enabling me to compare the characters clearly.

I compared the printing and the cursive writing. Mr. Best's *E* on the booking sheet included a frill. I removed the frill to obtain just the letter *E*. Sure enough, the structure of all the upper case *E*s was very similar.

Analysis of Writing Style

The Zodiac letters appear to have been written by an educated person who is capable of communicating clearly.

As evidenced by the quotation in the Exorcist letter (Appendix Exhibit 27), he was familiar with Gilbert and Sullivan's operetta *The Mikado*.

The use of cryptograms, especially those that are difficult to solve, is the sign of an educated person. The Zodiac sent many cryptograms to the newspapers. Only one was successfully solved.

Also, the grammar used by the Zodiac is the sign of an educated person.

Although exhibiting an educated writing style, the Zodiac appeared to intentionally misspell many words. Common words were misspelled in several letters. Examples of the following misspellings and more can be found in the letters in the Appendix.

- *Christmass* in the first Zodiac letter, the Lake Herman letter to the *San Francisco Chronicle*, *The San Francisco Examiner* and the *Vallejo Times-Herald*, the letter and envelope to Melvin Beli
- *drownding, extreamly, posibly*, and others in the letter to Melvin Beli
- *Fry* for Friday in the Lake Herman letter to the *San Francisco Chronicle*
- *motorcicles* in the letter after the murder of Paul Stein

Based on the observed intelligence of the Zodiac killer, these words may have been intentionally misspelled to make readers think the writer was illiterate.

Conclusion

Document examiners use nine levels for expressing the opinions which result from an examination. The opinions expressed in this report are defined as follows:

- ASTM Standard E1658 defines **strong probability** as, "The evidence is very persuasive, yet some critical feature or quality is missing so that an identification is not in order; however, the examiner is **virtually certain** that the questioned and known writings were written by the same individual. Examples—There is strong probability that the John Doe of the known material wrote the questioned material, or it is my opinion (or conclusion or determination) that the John Doe of the known material very probably wrote the questioned material."

- ASTM Standard E1658 defines **probable** as, "the evidence contained in the handwriting points rather strongly toward the questioned and known writings having been written by the same individual; however, it falls short of the 'virtually certain' degree of confidence."

- ASTM Standard E1658 defines **indications** as, "…a body of writing has few features which are of significance for handwriting comparison purposes, but those features are in agreement with another body of writing."

- ASTM Standard E1658 defines **elimination** as, "… the highest degree of confidence expressed by the document examiner in handwriting comparisons. By using this expression the examiner denotes no doubt in his opinion that the questioned and known writings were not written by the same individual."

The result of the comparison of the Zodiac's writings and the documents attributed to Earl Van Best Jr.'s writing is a rejection of the hypothesis that they were written by different people. The alternative hypothesis that they were written by the same person is accepted. There is a **strong probability** (virtually certain) Earl Van Best Jr. was the Zodiac Killer.

By examining the letters, envelopes and notes written by the Zodiac, I determined that there is a **strong probability** they were written by the same person with the exception of the 1978 letter to KHJ TV and the 1990 letter which are **eliminated** as being written by the same writer as the other Zodiac letters.

There are **indications** that the Red Phantom letter was written by the writer of the Zodiac letters.

It is **probable** that the letters written to the Riverside police, *The Press-Enterprise* and Mr. Bates subsequent to the 1967 Riverside murder were written by the person who wrote the Zodiac letters.

Comparison of the Zodiac letters, envelopes and notes with the marriage certificate between Earl Van Best Jr. and Judith Chandler, results in the professional opinion that there is a **strong probability** they were written by the same person.

Epilogue

A few days after Gary and Susan received my report, Susan called and asked, "Would you like to see the police sketches of Van and a photograph of him?" She had acquired two police sketches. The second was a revision made by the sketch artist after showing the first rendition to the witnesses.

"Of course I want to see them!" How could anyone resist being curious about such a sinister human being?

A few days later when I laid my eyes on the rather stark, staring images for the first time, a thought crossed my mind. "What will happen if I superimpose the police sketch onto the photograph of Van?" I thought seeing how well they matched would be interesting.

Using Photoshop I enlarged the police sketch proportionally. When I overlaid it onto the photo of Earl Van Best Jr. I was greeted by a final, bone-chilling surprise.

The photo and police sketch matched almost exactly—even the nose, ears, eyes, and horn rimmed glasses—even where the glasses sat on his face, just below the eyebrows.

Immediately I sent the composite to Susan. She was as horrified as I had been.

Figure 8 shows the police sketch of the Zodiac and the photograph of Earl Van Best Jr. side-by-side. Figure 9 shows the composite image of the sketch placed over the photograph. You decide.

Figure 8 – Police sketch of the Zodiac and Photograph of Earl Van Best Jr.

Figure 9 – Blue Zodiac Police Sketch is an Uncanny Likeness of Earl Van Best Jr.

Other Sources of Information on the Zodiac Killer

If you are interested in learning more about the history of the Zodiac killer, visit the following websites:

Websites about the Zodiac killer:

Zodiackiller.com

Zodiackillerfacts.com

Official website for the book, *The Most Dangerous Animal of All*:

Themostdangerousanimalofall.com

Appendix

 Q9 Consulting, Inc.

December 9, 2012

Susan Mustafa
Baton Rouge, LA

Re: **Compare writing of Earl Best Jr. with letters from the Zodiac Killer**
Document Examination Case Report No. 2012-31

Dear Ms. Mustafa:

You engaged my services to ascertain whether the writing or known writing of Earl Van Best Jr. identifies him as the writer of the letters and envelopes written by the Zodiac Killer.

I, Michael N. Wakshull, declare as follows:

All of the facts stated herein are personally known to me and if required to do so, I could and would testify to the truth thereof. The conclusions of my report are:

1. I've conducted a forensic handwriting analysis on copies of the Zodiac letters, comparing them to a copy of the marriage certificate between Earl Van Best Jr. and Judith Chandler, the writer of which you have identified as Earl Van Best jr.

2. I am virtually certain the writer of the marriage certificate between Earl Van Best Jr. and Judith Chandler is the same writer as the writer of the Zodiac letters.

3. I am virtually certain the writer of the marriage certificate between Earl Van Best Jr. and Mary Annette Player and the envelope addressed to *The Press-Enterprise* are the same writer.

4. I am virtually certain the writer of the marriage certificate between Earl Van Best Jr. and Edith Kos and the Joseph Bates envelope are the same writer.

5. There is a strong probability the writer of the Earl Van Best Jr. signature on the booking sheet is the writer of the envelope addressed to *The Press-Enterprise*

6. The *Channel Nine* letter was not authored by the same person who wrote the other Zodiac letters

7. There are indications the writer of the *Red Phantom* letter is the same person who wrote the other Zodiac letters

I declare under the penalty of perjury under the laws of the State of California that the foregoing is true and correct.

Executed this 9th day of December, 2012 at Temecula, CA.

If you have any questions about the findings of this report, please do not hesitate to contact me.

Sincerely,
Michael N. Wakshull

DOCUMENT EXAMINATION REPORT

Report Prepared For: Susan Mustafa
Re: Compare the writing of Earl Van Best Jr. with the writing of the Zodiac Killer
Report No.: 2012-31
Date: December 9, 2012

Document Examination Request

You engaged my services to ascertain whether the writing or known writing of Earl Van Best Jr. identifies him as the writer of the letters, envelopes and notes written by the Zodiac Killer.

Known Documents Examined – See Exhibits 1 - 4

Control Number	Document Date	Copy / Original	Type of Document	Exhibit #
K01	11-Jan-1962	Copy	Marriage certificate of Earl Van Best Jr. and Judith Chandler	Exhibit 1
K02	07-Aug-1957	Copy	Marriage certificate of Earl Van Best Jr. and Mary Player	Exhibit 2
K03	06-Jun-1966	Copy	Marriage certificate of Earl Van Best Jr. and Edith Kos	Exhibit 3
K04	27-Feb-1962	Copy	Booking sheet from San Francisco Jail	Exhibit 4

Questioned Documents Examined – See Exhibits 5 – 30, 42

Control Number	Date	Copy / Original	Type of Document	Exhibit #
Q01	30-Apr-1967	Copy	Envelope to Riverside Police	Exhibit 5
Q02	31-Jul-1969	Copy	Envelope to Vallejo Times-Herald	Exhibit 6
Q03	08-Nov-1969	Copy	Envelope to San Francisco Chronicle – 340 Cipher	Exhibit 7
Q04	13-Oct-1969	Copy	Envelope to San Francisco Chronicle – Stine murder	Exhibit 8
Q05	09-Nov-1969	Copy	Envelope to San Francisco Chronicle – Bus bomb letter	Exhibit 9
Q06	31-Jul-1969	Copy	Envelope to San Francisco Examiner – Lake Herman letter	Exhibit 10
Q07	30-Apr-1967	Copy	Letter to Joseph Bates – Riverside	Exhibit 11
Q08	31-Jul-1969	Copy	Lake Herman letter page 1 San Francisco Chronicle	Exhibit 12
Q09	31-Jul-1969	Copy	Lake Herman letter page 2 San Francisco Chronicle	Exhibit 13

Q10	31-Jul-1969	Copy	Lake Herman letter page 1 San Francisco Examiner	Exhibit 14
Q11	04-Aug-1969	Copy	First letter using Zodiac page 1 SF Examiner	Exhibit 15
Q12	04-Aug-1969	Copy	First letter using Zodiac page 2 San Francisco Examiner	Exhibit 16
Q13	13-Oct-1969	Copy	Stine murder letter San Francisco Chronicle	Exhibit 17
Q14	20-Dec-1969	Copy	Letter to Melvin Beli	Exhibit 18
Q15	26-Jun-1970	Copy	Button Cipher letter San Francisco Chronicle	Exhibit 19
Q16	24-Jul-1970	Copy	Kathleen Johns letter San Francisco Chronicle	Exhibit 20
Q17	26-July-1970	Copy	Little List letter page 1 San Francisco Chronicle	Exhibit 21
Q18	26-July-1970	Copy	Little List letter page 2 San Francisco Chronicle	Exhibit 22
Q19	26-July-1970	Copy	Little List letter page 3 San Francisco Chronicle	Exhibit 23
Q20	26-July-1970	Copy	Little List letter page 4 San Francisco Chronicle	Exhibit 24
Q21	26-July-1970	Copy	Little List letter San Francisco Chronicle page 5	Exhibit 25
Q22	13-Mar-1971	Copy	Blue Meannies letter to Los Angeles Times	Exhibit 26
Q23	29-Jan-1974	Copy	Exorcist letter to San Francisco Chronicle	Exhibit 27

Q24	08-May-1974	Copy	Citizen letter to San Francisco Chronicle	Exhibit 28
Q25	08-Jul-1974	Copy	Red Phantom letter to San Francisco Chronicle	Exhibit 29
Q26	02-May-1978	Copy	Letter to KHJ-TV in Los Angeles	Exhibit 30
Q27	30-Apr-1967	Copy	Envelope addressed to The Press-Enterprise	Exhibit 42
Q28	31-Jul-1969	Copy	Solved Cipher	Exhibit 43
Q29	20-Apr-1970	Copy	My Name Is Cipher	Exhibit 45
Q30	30-Apr-1967	Copy	Letter to The Press-Enterprise	Exhibit 47
Q31	08-Nov-1969	Copy	Thing letter	Exhibit 38
Q32	Dec-1990	Copy	Secret Pal card	Exhibit 48

Assumptions

- All known documents of Earl Van Best's writing are true reproductions of the original documents
- All letters, envelopes, and notes are true images of the original letters, envelopes, and notes sent by the Zodiac killer to people and organizations
- Judith Chandler observed Earl Van Best Jr. write all the entries on the marriage certificate (Exhibit 1) other than signatures of witnesses
- Earl Van Best Jr. signed the marriage certificate between him and Mary Annette Player
- Earl Van Best signed the marriage certificate between him and Edith Kos

- Earl Van Best Jr. signed the booking sheet

Limitations

- Original documents were not available for this document examiner to view
- The questioned documents from the Zodiac were taken from web sites
- The time between the writing of the known documents and the questioned documents is sufficient for a person to make changes to his normal handwriting
- The quantity of known writing of Earl Van Best Jr. is small

Method

Printed copies of the internet images were received by this document examiner from Susan Mustafa. Other images were extracted from the web sites www.zodiackiller.com and www.zodiackillerfacts.com. The images were extracted using Snagit software then placed into Adobe Photoshop.

The paper documents were scanned at 600 PPI on a Canon CanoScan 5600F digital scanner. The images were saved as TIFF format so as to retain detail.

The documents were analyzed, compared, and evaluated using visual techniques including magnification and digital imaging. Where applicable, ASTM forensic document examination standards were used. The standards used are

- ASTM E2290-07a Standard Guide for Examination of Handwritten Items
- ASTM E1658-04 Standard Terminology for Expressing Conclusions of Forensic Document Examiners

Adobe® Photoshop CS4® was used to compare documents side-by-side. Adobe Photoshop was used to create all exhibits. Snagit™ software was used to capture the Photoshop images and place the images into this report as Exhibits 1 – 48.

Due to the small quantity of known writing the examination was performed in a reverse manner. Normally the known writing (Earl Van Best Jr.) is examined to determine the common attributes of the writing. The questioned documents (Zodiac) are compared with the known documents to determine whether the common attributes of the known writing are present in the questioned writing and discover differences between the questioned and known writing. Since there were only four known writings and sixty questioned writings, the questioned writings were compared to determine whether they were written by a common writer. The questioned documents were treated in the manner known documents are normally treated. The known documents were treated as questioned documents for comparison. The result is the known documents were compared with the questioned documents to determine whether the common traits of the questioned documents are present in the known documents to determine whether the known writing aligns with the questioned writing.

Determine whether the Zodiac Killer letters were authored by the same person

All the letters and envelopes allegedly written by the Zodiac killer and those not directly identified as the Zodiac killer were laid out side-by-side for visual observation to discover whether unique characteristics exist among the writings. These unique characteristics are indicative of a possible common authorship as they define the uniqueness of the writer, rather than attributes of a commonly used writing system. Adobe Photoshop was used to perform a more detailed analysis of subjective visual common features among the Zodiac documents for the purpose of reducing subjective visual bias.

The Zodiac letters were examined for the unique characteristics found in the in the marriage certificate. The Zodiac letters and envelopes displaying the unique characteristics were selected for inclusion in this report as Exhibits 5 – 30, 38, 42, 43, 45, 46, 48. Some of the letters and envelopes that displayed these unique characteristics were not included in this report for the sake of brevity as additional exhibits would not alter the results of this report.

The common phrase, *This is the Zodiac speaking* was extracted from the letters containing this phrase and placed onto a Photoshop page (Exhibit 39) for comparison. The purpose is to determine the similarities and differences among the writings. The phrase *Rush to Editor* that appears on many envelopes was compared. Words that appear in several writings were compared. Examples are:

- bomb
- buttons
- The characters *est*
- The characters *San Fran*

Determine whether Earl Van Best wrote the Zodiac Killer letters and envelopes

This section assumes Judith Chandler is correct in stating she observed Earl Van Best Jr. write the entries in the marriage certificate between them. The purpose of this section is determination whether the person who wrote the entries in the marriage certificate between Earl Van Best Jr. and Judith Chandler wrote the Zodiac killer letters and envelopes.

The marriage certificate between Earl Van Best Jr. and Judith Chandler (Exhibit 1) was examined for unusual characteristics unique to the writer. These characteristics are letter formations and permutations of letter sequences. A permutation is a specific order in which the letters are written. An example is *San* is a different permutation than *Sna*.

The unique writing portions of the marriage certificate between Earl Van Best Jr. and Judith Chandler that had matching entries in the Zodiac writings. These were extracted from the certificate using Adobe Photoshop software and placed onto separate pages. The entries extracted were:

1. Capital *J*, Exhibit 31
2. Letter sequence *ss*, Exhibit 32
3. Capital letter *E*, Exhibits 33 & 34 & 46
4. Lower case *n*, Exhibit 35
5. Letter sequence *est*, Exhibits 36, 37
6. Letter sequence *San Fran*, Exhibit 40
7. Letter sequence *Calif*, Exhibit 41
8. Upper case *M*, Exhibit 44
9. *elf* and *of*, Exhibit 37

Extraneous markings were removed from the writing using the eraser tool in Photoshop. Extraneous markings can potentially bias the results due to confusion whether the extraneous markings are part of the writing being compared with another writing. Writing from different sources was color coded for identification. The writings were superimposed onto each other for comparison of similarities and differences between the presumed known writing of Earl Van Best Jr. and the questioned writing of the Zodiac killer.

The letter Q followed by a number (for example Q12) is used to indicate a questioned writing sample.

The *E* from the marriage certificate between Earl Van Best Jr. and Mary Player (Exhibit 2), the marriage certificate between Earl Van Best Jr. and Edith Kos (Exhibit 3), and the booking sheet (Exhibit 4) were compared with the questioned documents Q07 (Exhibit 11) and Q27 (Exhibit 42). The comparison is displayed in Exhibit 33. These comparisons were made because the signatures in the marriage certificates are cursive and the writing in Exhibit 42 is cursive. Although Exhibit 11 is printed, the formation of the capital *E* is similar to the cursive *E* in the marriage certificates.

The symbol at the bottom of Q30 (Exhibit 46) was examined to determine whether it is a letter *Z* or a cryptogram (Exhibit 47). The symbol was extracted from Q30 and enlarged using Photoshop. The symbol was rotated 90 degrees clockwise. The clockwise rotation was flipped 180 degrees horizontally. A comparison of the symbol at the bottom of Q30 was made with the cursive *E* in *Earl* in Exhibit 2, Exhibit 3 and Exhibit 4. The symbol was then rotated 90 degrees counter-clockwise and examined.

Measurements were made of angles and heights using the measurement tool in Photoshop. Exhibit 33 shows an example of using the angle measurements for comparison.

Results

Huber and Hedrick[1] identified 21 attributes of writing for comparison to determine authenticity of signatures. The attributes used in this examination are:

1. Arrangement
2. Class of Allograph

---

[1] Huber, R. &Hedrick, A.M. Handwriting Identification, Facts and Fundamentals. (Boca Raton: CRC Press, 1999) p. 136-138.

3. Connections
4. Design of Allographs
5. Dimensions
6. Slant and slope
7. Spacings interword and intraword
8. Abbreviations
9. Alignment to a baseline
10. Commencements and terminations
11. Diacritics and punctuation
12. Embellishments
13. Legibility and writing quality
14. Line continuity
15. Line quality
16. Pen control
17. Writing movement
18. Consistency or natural variation
19. Persistency
20. Lateral expansion
21. Word proportions

Similarities observed between the Zodiac letters and the marriage certificate between Earl Van Best Jr. and Judith Chandler

1. The **arrangement** of the writing is similar across the questioned documents except for Exhibits 11 and 30
2. **Class of allograph** is the same (printing), except the envelope to *The Press-Enterprise* (Exhibit 42) which is cursive.

3. The **connections** do not exist because the writing is printed. The cursive signatures in K02, K03 and K04 were not compared with the printed letters

4. **Design of Allographs** are similar

5. The **dimensions** are similar

6. The **slant angle** is similar

7. The **spacing** interword and intraword is similar yet the insufficiency of writing multiple words and no line-to-line writing in the known documents does not afford the ability to fully examine this attribute.

8. **Abbreviations** are not used in the marriage certificate so no comparison was made for this attribute.

9. **Alignment to a baseline** is similar. The baseline is the base of the writing rather than a line on which a signature is written. The baseline of the questioned and known writings is virtually horizontal with little deviation from the horizontal.

10. **Connections and terminations** were not examined as this is printing without connections between letters

11. **Diacritics and punctuation** are not used in the marriage certificate. This attribute was not examined.

12. The letters and envelopes written simply without **embellishments.** Therefore this attribute was not considered in this examination.

13. The writing is written **legibly and writing quality is similar except for Exhibits 11 and 30.**

14. **Line continuity** appears similar in the marriage certificate and the Zodiac letters. Since the documents are not original documents this attribute cannot be adequately measured.

15. The **line quality** (thickness, pressure, anomalies) is similar in the known and questioned signatures

16. The writer appears to demonstrate similar **pen control** across the documents. Since these are copies the pressure is difficult to ascertain with certainty.

17. The **writing movement** is similar across the documents

18. The writing appears to show similar **consistency and natural variation** across the documents. This attribute is elaborated in the section "Assessment of Variability".

19. **Persistency** is demonstrated in the repetition of common identifying tendencies such as the formation of the pair *ss* in Exhibit 32 and lower-case *n* in the appearance of a *u*. Exhibit 35.

20. The **lateral expansion** appears similar in the marriage certificate and the Zodiac letters. This attribute is difficult to clearly specify since the writing quantity on the marriage certificate is too little to determine whether it would persist across a larger space.

21. The **word proportions** are the proportions of the upper case letters to the lower case (middle zone) letters.

Differences between the Zodiac letters and the marriage certificate between Earl Van Best Jr. and Judith Chandler

1. The lower case *y* is formed differently in the marriage certificate (Exhibit 1) than in the Zodiac letters.
2. The lower case *d* is formed differently in the marriage certificate than in the Zodiac letters.
3. The slant of the capital letter *M* is generally more vertical than in Exhibit 1 (see Exhibit 44). An exception is the *M* in the Blue Meannies letter (Exhibit 26).
4. The Zodiac letter from May 2, 1978 to KHJ-TV does not have similar characteristics found in the other letters and envelopes
5. The Red Phantom letter may be a disguised writing from the author of the other Zodiac letters. Some of the 21 attributes are found in the letter yet there is insufficient evidence to determine whether it is from the same writer.

Overview of the comparison analysis

Exhibit 31

The capital letter *J* in *January* and *Judith* is virtually identical with the three instances of the letter in the Zodiac letters. The characters *J* were proportionally sized to approximately the same heights using Photoshop. The *J*s from the Zodiac letters were colored to differentiate them from the marriage certificate entries. The colored entries were superimposed onto the black entries from the marriage certificate. The result is the characters have the same construction and slant in the questioned Zodiac writing and the known writing.

Exhibit 32

The shape of the *ss* is similar between the marriage certificate and the Zodiac letters. The top line shows the *ss* from "Nilsson" in the marriage certificate. The entry on the right has been set to red 50% opacity. The color was changed from red to a light green as this provides a better offset to the questioned writing than the light red. The spacing and shape of the letters is almost identical in all except the "Citizen" entry. The shape in the "Citizen" entry is similar to the marriage certificate. The inter-character spacing is different.

Exhibit 33

This exhibit compares the cursive form capital letter *E* in the envelope addressed to *The Press-Enterprise* newspaper (Exhibit 42) and the letter to Joseph Bates (Exhibit 11) with the cursive style *E* in Earl Van Best's signature on Exhibit 2 and Exhibit 3. Extraneous marks were removed to retain only the letter *E* for comparison.

The characters were colored differently to differentiate them when they are placed on top of each other for comparison. When the vertical line was removed from the *E* in *MORE* from the Bates letter (Exhibit 11) and the lead-in stroke was removed from the Kos marriage certificate (Exhibit 3) signature, the two superimpose almost perfectly, other than the base stroke.

The bottom row shows a comparison of the *E* from the envelope to *The Press-Enterprise* with the known writing.

A comparison was made by superimposing all known *E* characters onto each other for comparison. The structure and slants are all within expected variability of the same writer.

The measurement tool in Photoshop was used to measure the angle of slant of each character. The slant of *The Press-Enterprise* envelope letter *E* is within the demonstrated variability of the known writing.

Exhibit 34

This exhibit compares the printed capital *E* in the marriage certificate to Judith Chandler with the printed *E* in the Zodiac letters. The characters were colored differently to distinguish them from each other when superimposed. The two entries were made from the *San Francisco Examiner* envelope to show the variability of the writing in the same session.

The comparison shows a virtually identical structure and slant of the characters. The only prominent difference is the *E* in *Examiner* in row 3. The other *E* on the same envelope in row 2 demonstrates the same slant as the known writing.

Exhibit 35

The formation of the lower case *n* in the marriage certificate to Chandler is a unique form that looks more like a lower case *u* than an *n*. Examples of this unusual construction were extracted from several of the Zodiac letters showing this is a strong probability they were all written by the same person.

Exhibit 36

The characters *est* are present in the name *Best* on the marriage certificate to Chandler. There are several occurrences of this pattern in the Zodiac letters. The occurrences in the Zodiac letters were colored then placed onto the *est* from the known writing from the marriage certificate to determine similarity. The spacing and structure of the questioned Zodiac writing is within the expected variability of the same writer of the marriage certificate.

Exhibit 37

This exhibit compares the marriage certificate to Chandler with the Exorcist letter, Exhibit 27. When the extracted text is superimposed onto its respective entry, the structures of the characters and spacing are within the expected variability of the same writer.

Exhibit 39

This exhibit shows the extraction of the words *This is the Zodiac Speaking* from each letter that contains this phrase. All show similar spacing and are within expected variability, except the Channel Nine entry (first from last). In the Channel Nine entry the formation of the letter *d* in Zodiac is a Greek form that is not seen in any of the other writings, the height proportions differ, the design of allographs is different, and the spacing is different from the other Zodiac writings.

Exhibit 40

This exhibit compares the two instances of writing *San Fran* on the marriage certificate to Chandler with the addresses on the envelopes. The entries on the marriage certificate were colored red and blue. These were then superimposed over the entries from the envelope. The size of the *S* is larger in the marriage certificate relative to the other characters on the envelopes. The spacing between "San" and *Fran* is within expected variability when compared with the envelopes. The *Fran* is within expected variability of one person having written the documents.

Exhibit 41

This exhibit compares the *Calif* in California on the marriage certificate to Chandler with the entries on the envelopes. The spacing, size, character construction and slant are all within expected variability of one writer except the letter to the Riverside Police Department.

Exhibit 44

This exhibit compares the capital letter *M* in the marriage certificate between Earl Van Best and Judith Chandler with the instances of the capital *M* in the Zodiac letters. The shape and slant of the letter are unique. The letter shows intra-writer variability in the depth of the connector between the vertical sides of the character. The shallow roundedness is a distinctive feature of the character. The slant is virtually the same in the Blue Meannies letter (Exhibit 26). The shallow roundedness of the connector is similar, especially compared with the *M* in *Minister* in the certificate. The width of the characters is similar between the certificate and the *M* in *Minister* and *Methodist*. Although the width of the *M* in Birdie M. is narrower than the Blue Meannies letter, the slant is virtually the same."

The other instances of the letter *M* in the Zodiac letters are slanted vertically which differs from the right slant in the marriage certificate. The width of the *M* in "Minister" is virtually the same as the width of the *M* found in the Zodiac letters. The width of the *M* in *Methodist* is virtually the same as the width of the *M* in Blue Meannies, Solved Cipher and Button Cipher Map letters.

Exhibit 47

This exhibit examines the symbol at the bottom of the letter to the Riverside Press-Enterprise (Exhibit 46). The symbol appears to be the letter *Z* written with a wavy top horizontal line. When the symbol is enlarged then rotated 90 degrees counter-clockwise it has the appearance of the letters *EV* using a Greek style *E* or epsilon. This is the form of *E* used in *Earl* in the signatures on the marriage certificates to Edith Kos (Exhibit 3) and Annette Player (Exhibit 2) and the arrest booking sheet (Exhibit 4).

When the symbol is rotated 90 degrees clockwise it has the appearance of a cursive letter *B* with the top portion of the *B* separated from the up-and-down stroke.

When this clockwise rotation is flipped 180 degrees the Greek style *E* is apparent. The appearance of the *E* is almost identical with the *E* in *Earl* in the Kos marriage certificate signature. The structure is similar in shape and form with the *E* in the marriage certificate to Player and the arrest booking sheet.

The symbol appears to be a cryptogram rather than the letter *Z*.

Conclusion

ASTM E1658-04 Standard Terminology for Expressing Conclusions of Forensic Document

Examiners has been used in the preparation of the opinions in this report. ASTM provides the
following nine-level scale for expressing conclusions:
- identification
- strong probability
- probable
- indications
- no conclusion
- indications did not
- probably did not
- strong probability did not
- elimination

ASTM Standard 1658 defines **strong probability** as, "The evidence is very persuasive, yet some critical feature or quality is missing so that an identification is not in order; however, the examiner is virtually certain that the questioned and known writings were written by the same individual. Examples—There is strong probability that the John Doe of the known material wrote the questioned material, or it is my opinion (or conclusion or determination) that the John Doe of the known material very probably wrote the questioned material."

ASTM Standard 1658 defines **probable** as, "The the evidence contained in the handwriting points
rather strongly toward the questioned and known writings having been written by the same individual; however, it falls short of the ' virtually certain' degree of confidence."

ASTM Standard 1658 defines **indications** as, "a body of writing has few features which are of significance for handwriting comparison purposes, but those features are in agreement with another body of writing."

ASTM Standard 1658 defines elimination as, "… the highest degree of confidence expressed by the document examiner in handwriting comparisons. By using this expression the examiner denotes no doubt in his opinion that the questioned and known writings were not written by the same individual."

A copy of this examiner's curriculum vitae is attached along with demonstrative exhibits and
copies of the documents examined. If court testimony is required, please contact the undersigned.

I, Michael N. Wakshull, declare as follows:

All of the facts stated herein are personally known to me and if required to do so, I could and would testify to the truth thereof. The conclusions of my report are:

Based upon the aforementioned examination results and available evidence, there is evidence to support the opinion:

1. There is a **strong probability** the writer of the marriage certificate between Earl Van Best Jr. and Judith Chandler is the same writer as the writer of the Zodiac letters.
2. There is a **strong probability** the writer of the marriage certificate between Earl Van Best and Mary Annette Player and the envelope addressed to the Press-Enterprise are the same person.
3. There is a **strong probability** the writer of the marriage certificate between Earl Van Best Jr. and Edith Kos and the Joseph Bates envelope are the same person.
4. It is probable that the writer of the Earl Van Best Jr. signature on the booking sheet is the writer of the envelope addressed to the Press-Enterprise
5. The Channel Nine letter (Exhibit 30) is **eliminated** as the same person who wrote the other Zodiac letters
6. There are **indications** the Red Phantom letter was authored by the same person who wrote the other Zodiac letters

I declare under the penalty of perjury under the laws of the State of California that the foregoing is true and correct.

Executed this 9th day of December, 2012 at Temecula, CA.

Sincerely,

Michael N. Wakshull MS, CQE
Q9 Consulting, Inc.
Document Examiner

Exhibits

BOOK 341 PAGE 200

No. 552997

Marriage Certificate

Filed at request of __REV.E.M.FLIGER__

State of Nevada } ss.
County of Washoe }

Recorded __JAN 11 1962__
Records of Washoe County, Nevada
Indexed ___✓___ __Delle B Wyse__
County Recorder

This is to Certify that the undersigned __Minister of St. Paul's__ __Methodist Church, Reno__ did on the __5th__ day of __January__ A.D. 19 __62__ join in lawful Wedlock __Earl V. Best, Jr.__ of __San Francisco__ State of __California__ and __Judith E. Chandler__ of __San Francisco__ State of __California__ with their mutual consent in the presence of __Birdie M. Nilsson__ and __A.S. Belford__ who were witnesses.

__Birdie M Nilsson__
signature of witness
__A.S Belford__
signature of witness

__Edward M. Fliger__

Exhibit 1- K01, Marriage Certificate—Earl Van Best Jr. and Judith Chandler January 5, 1962

Exhibit 2 - K02, Marriage to Mary Annette Player – August 7, 1957

Exhibit 3 - K03, Marriage to Edith Kos – June 6, 1966

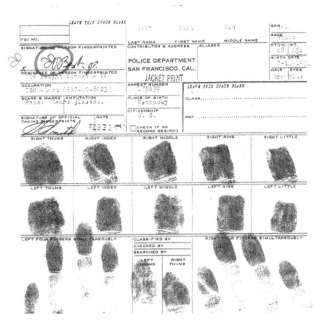

Exhibit 4 - K04, Booking Sheet San Francisco – February 22, 1962

Exhibit 5 – Q01, Riverside PD Envelope – April 30, 1967

Exhibit 6 - Q02, Vallejo *Times-Herald* Envelope – July 31, 1969

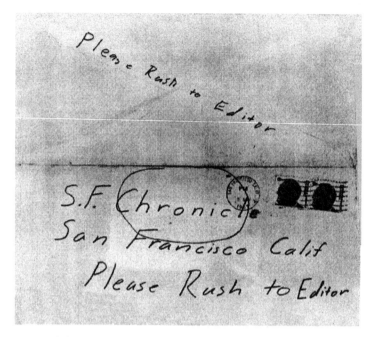

Exhibit 7 - Q03, 340 cipher envelope to Chronicle –
November 8, 1969

Exhibit 8 - Q04, Stein Letter Envelope – October 13, 1969

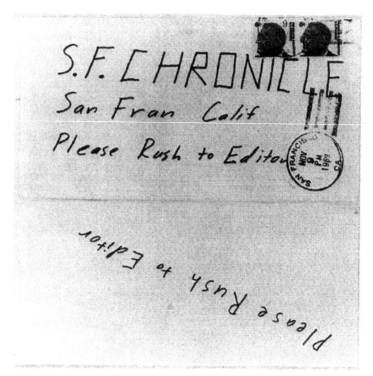

Exhibit 9 - Q05, Bus Bomb Letter – November 9, 1969

Exhibit 10 – Q06, Lake Herman *San Francisco Examiner* **Editor Envelope – July 31, 1969**

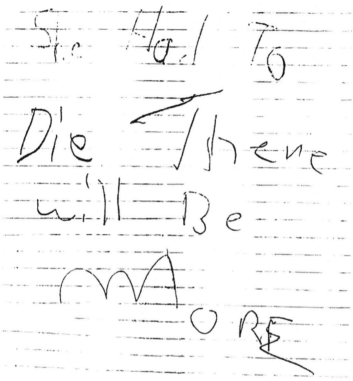

Exhibit 11 - Q07, Letter to *The Press-Enterprise* – April 30, 1967

Dear Editor

This is the murderer of the
2 teenagers last Christmass
at Lake Herman & the girl
on the 4th of July near
the golf course in Vallejo
To prove I killed them I
shall state some facts which
only I & the police know.
Christmass

  1 Brand name of ammo
    Super X
  2 10 shots were fired
  3 the boy was on his back
    with his feet to the car
  4 the girl was on her right
    side feet to the west
4th July

  1 girl was wearing patterned
    slacks
  2 The boy was also shot in
    the knee.
  3 Brand name of ammo was
    Western

Exhibit 12 - Q08, Lake Herman Letter to The *San Francisco Chronicle* Page 1 – July 31, 1969

79

Here is part of a cipher the
other 2 parts of this cipher are
being mailed to the editors of
the Vallejo times + SF Exam
iner.

I want you to print this cipher
on the front page of your
paper. In this cipher is my
idenity.

If you do not print this cipher
by the afternoon of Fry. 1st of
Aug 69, I will go on a kill ram-
page Fry. night. I will cruse
around all weekend killing lone
people in the night then more
on to kill again, untill I end
up with a dozen people over
the weekend.

Exhibit 13 - Q09, Lake Herman Letter to *The San Francisco Chronicle* Page 2 – July 31, 1969

Dear Editor

I am the killer of the 2 teenagers
last christmass at Lake Herman &
the girl last 4th of July. To prove
this I shall state some facts which
only I + the police know.
Christmass
1 brand name of ammo – Super X
2 10 shots fired
3 Boy was on his back with feet to
  car
4 Girl was lyeing on right side
  feet to west
4th of July
1 girl was wearing pattened pants
2 boy was also shot in knee
3 ammo was made by Western

Here is a cipher or that is part
of one. The other 2 parts are
being mailed to the Vallejo Times +
S.F. Chronicle

I want you to print this cipher on the front page by
Fry afternoon Aug 1-69 . If you

Exhibit 14 – Q10, Lake Herman Letter to The *San Francisco Examiner* Page 1 – July 31, 1969

Dear Editor
This is the Zodiac speaking.
In answer to your asking for
more details about the good
times I have had in Vallejo,
I shall be very happy to
supply even more material.
By the way, are the police
haveing a good time with the
code? If not, tell them to cheer
up; when they do crack it
they will have me.
On the 4th of July
I did not open the car door, The
window was rolled down all ready.
The boy was origionaly sitting in
the front seat when I began
fireing. When I fired the first
shot at his head, he leaped
backwards at the same time
thus spoiling my aim. He ended
ed up on the back seat then
the floor in back thrashing out
very violently with his legs;
thats how I shot him in the

**Exhibit 15 - Q11, First Letter That Mentions Zodiac page
1 – August 4, 1969**

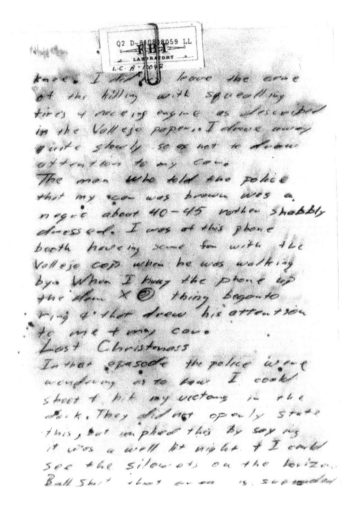

Exhibit 16 – Q12, First Letter That Mentions Zodiac page 2 – August 4, 1969

This is the Zodiac speaking.
I am the murderer of the
taxi driver over by
Washington St & Maple St last
night, to prove this here is
a blood stained piece of his
shirt. I am the same man
who did in the people in the
north bay area.
The S.F. Police could have caught
me last night if they had
searched the park properly
instead of holding road races
with their motor cicles seeing who
could make the most noise. The
cop driver should have just
parked their cars & sat there
quietly waiting for me to come
out of cover.
School children make nice targ-
ets, I think I shall wipe out
a school bus some morning. Just
shoot out the front tire & then
pick off the kiddies as they come
bouncing out.

Exhibit 17 - Q13, Letter Sent After Stein Murder – October
13, 1969

Dear Melvin

This is the Zodiac speaking I
wish you a happy Christmass.
The one thing I ask of you is
this, please help me. I cannot
reach out for help because of
this thing in me wont let me.
I am finding it extreamly dif-
icult to hold it in check I am
afraid I will loose control
again and take my nineth &
posibly tenth victom. Please
help me I am drownding, At
the moment the children are
safe from the bomb because
it is so massive to dig in & the
triger mech requires much wonk
to get it adjusted just right. But
if I hold back too long from
no nine I will loose ~~complet~~ all
controol of my self & set the
bomb up. Please help me I can
not remain in control for much

**Exhibit 18 - Q14, Letter to attorney Melvin Beli --
December 20, 1969**

This is the Zodiac speaking

I have become very upset with
the people of San Fran Bay
Area. They have _not_ complied
with my wishes for them to
wear some nice ⊕ buttons.
I promiced to punish them
if they didnot comply, by
anilating a full School Buss.
But now school is out for
the summer, so I panished
them in an another way.
I shot a man sitting in
a parked car with a .38.

⊕-12   SFPD-O

The Map coupled with this
code will tell you whoe the
bomb is set. You have untill
next Fall to dig it up. ⊕

C △ J I ■ O 人 ⅃ A M ⅂ ▲ Ω O R T G
X ☉ F D V ⊂ ▣ H C E L ⊕ P W △

Exhibit 19 – Q15, Button Cipher Letter –– June 26, 1970

This is the Zodiac speaking

I am rather unhappy because
you people will not wear some
nice ⌀ buttons. So I now
have a little list, starting with
the woeman + her baby that I
gave a rather intersting ride
fo- a coupple howers one
evening a few months back that
ended in my burning her
car where I found them.

Exhibit 20 – Q16, Letter after Kathleen Johns attempt – July 24, 1970

This is the Zodiac speaking

Being that you will not wear
some nice ⊕ buttons, how about
wearing some nasty ⊕ buttons.
Or any type of ⊕ buttons that
you can think up. If you do
not wear any type of ⊕
buttons I shall (on top of every
thing else) torture all 13
of my slaves that I have
wateing for me in Paradice.
Some I shall tie over ant hills
and watch them scream + twich
and squirm. Others shall have
pine splinters driven under their
nails + then burned. Others shall
be placed in cages + fed salt
beef untill they are gorged then
I shall listen to their pleass
for water and I shall laugh at
them. Others will hang by
their thumbs + barn in the
sam then I will rub them down

Exhibit 21 – Q17, Little List Page 1 Sent to The *San Francisco Chronicle* – July 26, 1970

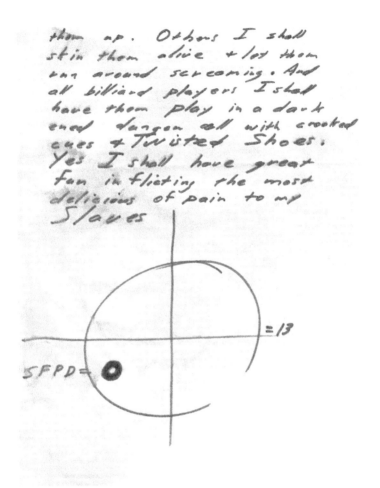

Exhibit 22 – Q18, Little List Page 2 Sent to The *San Francisco Chronicle* – July 26, 1970

As some day it may hapen
that a victom must be found.
I've got a little list. I've
got a little list, of society
offenders who might well be
underground who would never
be missed who would never be
missed. There is the pest-
ulentual nucences who whrite
for autographs, all people who
have flabby hands and irritat-
ing laughs. All children who
are up in dates and implore
you with implatt. All people
who are shakeing hands shake
hands like that. And all third
persons who with unspoiling
take thoes who insist. They'd
none of them be missed. They'd
none of them be missed. There's
the banjo seranader and
the others of his race and
the piano orginast I got him
on the list. All people who

Exhibit 23 – Q19, Little List Page 3 Sent to The *San Francisco Chronicle* – July 26, 1970

in your face, they would
never be missed They would
never be missed And the
Idiout whe phrases with in-
thusastic tone of centuries
but this and every country but
his own. And the lady from
the provences who dress like
a guy whe doesn't cry and
the singurly abnomily the
girl who never kissed. I don't
think she would be missed
Im share she wouldn't be
missed. And that nice impriest
that is rather rife the judic-
ial hummerest I've got him on
the list All funny fellows, com-
mic men and clowns of private
life. They'd none of them be
missed. They'd none of them be
missed. And uncompromiseing
kind such as wachamacallit,
thingmebob, and likewise, well
-nevermind, and tut tut tut tut,
and whatshisname, and you know

Exhibit 24 – Q20, Little List Sent to The *San Francisco Chronicle* Page 4 – July 26, 1970

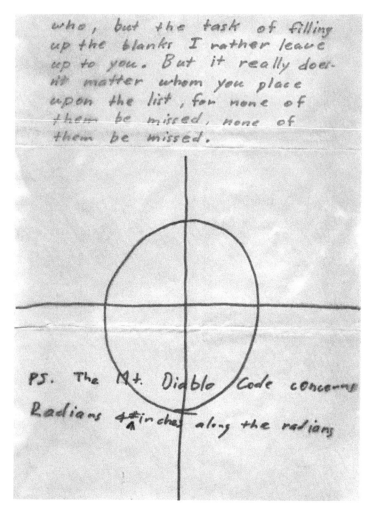

who, but the task of filling
up the blanks I rather leave
up to you. But it really does-
n't matter whom you place
upon the list, for none of
them be missed, none of
them be missed.

PS. The Mt. Diablo Code concerns
Radians 4#inches along the radians

Exhibit 25 – Q21, Little List Sent to The *San Francisco Chronicle* Page 5 –- July 26, 1970

This is the Zodiac speaking
Like I have always said
I am crack proof. If the
Blue Meannies are ever
going to catch me, they had
best get off their fat asses
& do something. Because the
longer they fiddle & fart
around, the more slaves
I will collect for my after
life. I do have to give them
credit for stumbling across
my river-side activity, but
they are only finding the
easy ones, there are a hell
of a lot more down there.
The reason that I'm writing
to the Times is this, They
dont bury me on the back page

Exhibit 26 – Q22, Blue Meannies Letter To *Los Angeles Times*
—March 13, 1971

I saw + think "The Exorcist"
was the best saterical com-
idy that I have ever seen.

Signed, yours truley :

He plunged him self into
the billowy wave
and an echo arose from
the sucides grove
    tit willo   tit willo
       tit willo

Ps. if I do not see this
note in your paper, I
will do something nasty,
which you know I'm capable of
doing
    !

Me - 37

SFPD - O

Exhibit 27 – Q23, Exorcist Letter To The *San Francisco Chronicle* **–- January 29, 1974**

Michael N. Wakshull, CQE, MSc

Sirs- I would like to
express ~~on~~ my ~~content~~
consternation concerning
your poor taste & lack of
sympathy for the public, as
evidenced by your running
of the ads for the movie
"Badlands," featuring the
blurb - "In 1959 most people
were killing time. Kit & Holly
were killing people." In
light of recent events, this
kind of murder-glorification
can only be deplorable at
best (not that glorification of
violence was ever justifiable)
why don't you show some
concern for public sensibilities
& cut the ad?

A citizen

Exhibit 28 – Q24, Citizen Letter to The *San Francisco Chronicle* — May 8, 1974

Editor —
Put Marco back in the Hell-hole
from whence it came — he has
a serious psychological disorder —
always needs to feel superior. I
suggest you refer him to a shrink.
Meanwhile, cancel the Count Marco
column. Since the Count can
write anonymously, so can I ———
the Red Phantom
(red with rage)

Exhibit 29 – Q25, Red Phantom Letter to The *San Francisco Chronicle* –- July 8, 1974

Dear Channel Nine;

This is the Zodiac speaking. You people in LA are in for a treat. In the next three weeks you are finally gona have something good to report. I have decided to begin killing again — PLEASE hold the app lause. Nothing is going to happen until I do. You people just won't let me have it Any other way. I plan to kill five people in the next three weeks (1) Chief piggy Tarrel Oates (2) Ex Chief piggy Ed Davis (3) Pat Boone — his theocratic crap is a obscenity to the rest of the world. (4) Also Eldrige Cleaver — the niggers gotta get their 20% quota — after all. And Susan Atkins — The Judas of the Manson Family. She's gona get hers now. Hey — — — you actors — this is your lucky break. Remember — whoever plays me has his work cut out for him. See you in the News!

Exhibit 30 – Q26, Letter To *KHJ-TV* Los Angeles –- May 2, 1978

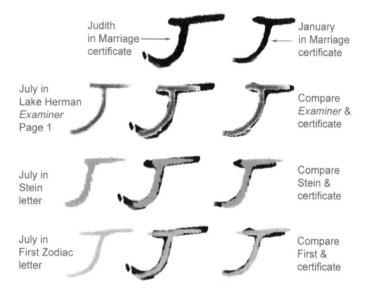

Judith in Marriage certificate → ← January in Marriage certificate

July in Lake Herman *Examiner* Page 1 — Compare *Examiner* & certificate

July in Stein letter — Compare Stein & certificate

July in First Zodiac letter — Compare First & certificate

Exhibit 31 – Compare Letter *J* with Marriage Certificate to Judith

Exhibit 32 – Compare Letters *ss* with Marriage Certificate to Judith

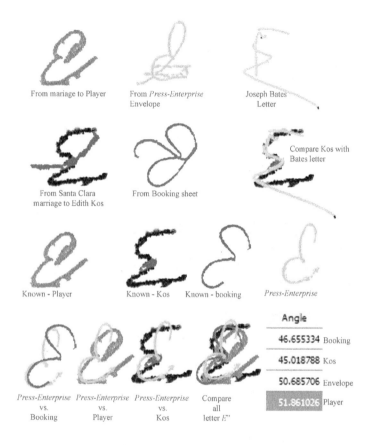

Exhibit 33 – Compare Capital *E* with Marriage Certificates to Player and Kos

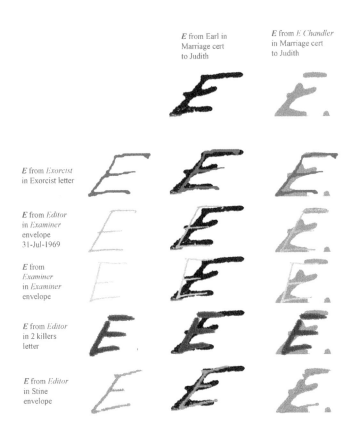

Exhibit 34 – Compare Capital *E* with Marriage Certificate to Judith

Compare Lower Case *n*

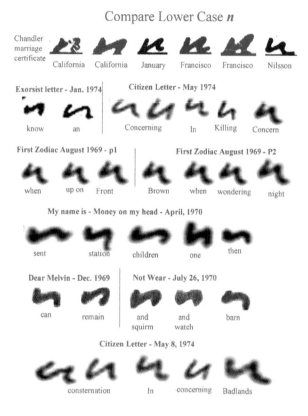

Exhibit 35 – Compare letter *n* with Marriage Certificate to Judith

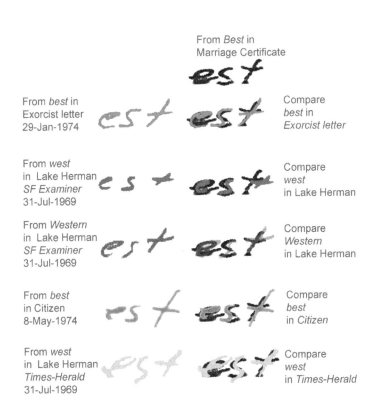

Exhibit 36 – Compare Letters *est* with Marriage Certificate to Judith

No. 552997

Marriage Certificate

Filed at request of REV.E.M.FLIGER

State of Nevada |
County of Washoe } ss.

Recorded JAN 11 1962
Records of Washoe County, Nevada
Indexed ✓ _Delle B Guy_
County Recorder

This is to Certify that the undersigned _Minister of St. Paul's Methodist Church, Reno_ did on the _5th_ day of _January_ A.D. 19 62 join in lawful Wedlock _Earl V. Best, Jr._ of _San Francisco_ State of _California_ and _Judith E. Chandler_ of _San Francisco_ State of _California_ with their mutual consent in the presence of _Birdie M. Nilsson_ and _A.S. Belford_ who were witnesses.

Birdie M Nilsson   _Edward M Fliger_
signature of witness
A.S Belford
signature of witness

From *best* in
Exorcist letter

From *Best* in
Marriage cert

Superimposed onto
each other

of from
Exorcist letter

of from
Marriage cert

Superimposed onto
each other

elf from *self*
in Exorcist letter

elf from
Belford in
Marriage cert

Superimposed onto
each other

**Exhibit 37 – Compare the Exorcist Letter With the
Marriage Certificate to Judith**

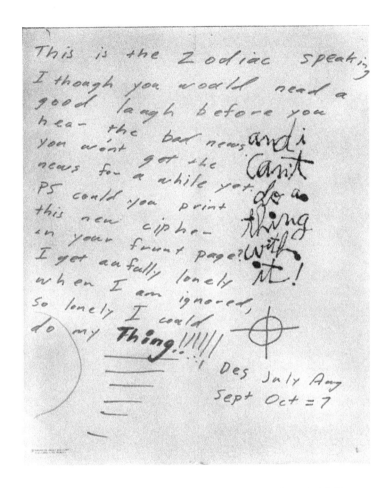

Exhibit 38 – Q31, Thing letter – November 8, 1969

This is the Zodiac speaking	Thing
This is the Zodiac speaking	Little List page 1
This is the Zodiac speaking	Blue Meannies
This is the Zodiac speaking	Button cipher
This is the Zodiac speaking	Dear Melvin
This is the Zodiac speaking	Kathleen Johns
This is the Zodiac speaking.	First Zodiac letter
This is the Zodiac speaking	Bus Bomb
This is the Zodiac speaking	My Name Is
This is the Zodiac speaking.	Channel Nine
This is the Zodiac speaking.	Stine Letter

Exhibit 39 – Compare *This is the Zodiac Speaking* **Across the Zodiac Letters**

Exhibit 40 – Compare *San Fran* on the Zodiac Letters With the Marriage Certificate to Judith

Exhibit 41 – Compare *Calif* on the Zodiac Letters With the Marriage Certificate to Judith

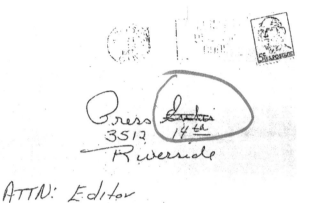

Exhibit 42 - Q27, Envelope addressed to *The Press-Enterprise*
– April 30, 1967

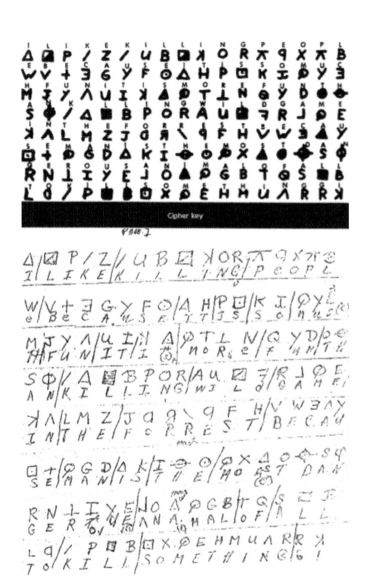

Exhibit 43 – Q28, Solved Cipher Vallejo *Times-Herald* Solved Cipher – July 31, 1969

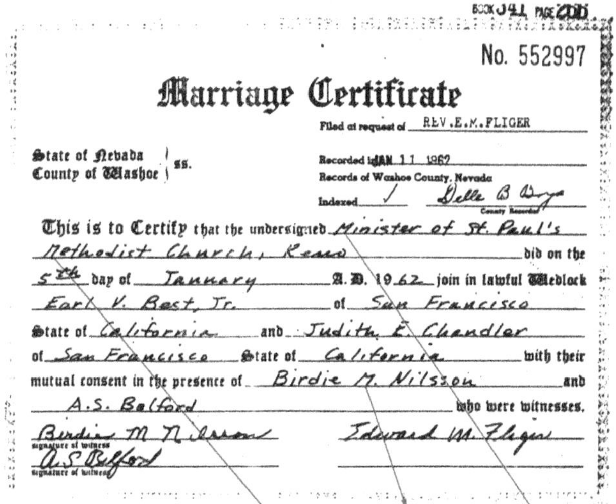

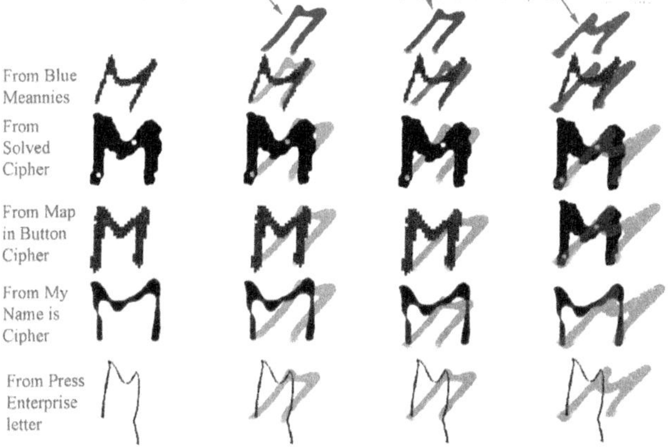

Exhibit 44 – Compare the Letter *M* in Zodiac Letters With the Marriage Certificate to Judith

This is the Zodiac speaking
By the way have you cracked
the last cipher I sent you?.
My name is ——

A E N ⊕ ⊗ K ⊙ M ⊘ ⅃ N A M

I am mildly cerous as to how
much money you have on my
head now. I hope you do not
think that I was the one
who wiped out that blue
meannie with a bomb at the
cop station. Even though I talked
about killing school children with
one. It just wouldn't doo to
move in on someone elses teritory.
But there is more glory in killing
a cop then a cid because a cop
con shoot back. I have killed
ten people to date. It would
have been a lot more except
that my bas bomb was a dod.
I was swamped out by the
rain we had a while back.

Exhibit 45 – Q29, *My Name Is* **Cipher**

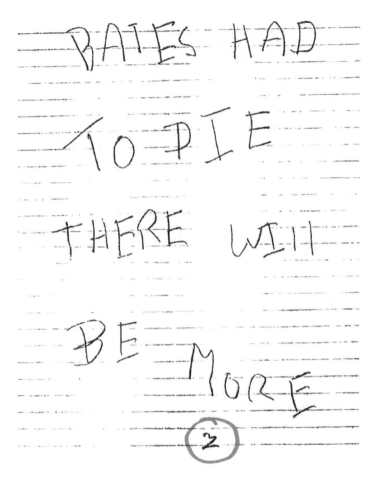

Exhibit 46 – Q29, Letter to *The Press-Enterprise* After Bates Murder – April 30, 1967

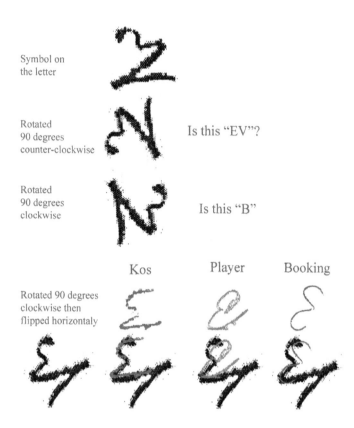

Symbol on
the letter

Rotated
90 degrees
counter-clockwise

Is this "EV"?

Rotated
90 degrees
clockwise

Is this "B"

Kos   Player   Booking

Rotated 90 degrees
clockwise then
flipped horizontaly

**Exhibit 47 – Compare the Cursive *E* from *Earl* to the
Symbol on *The Press-Enterprise* Letter**

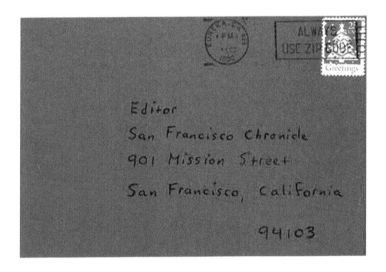

Exhibit 48 – Q32, *Secret Pal Card* to *San Francisco Chronicle* – December 1990

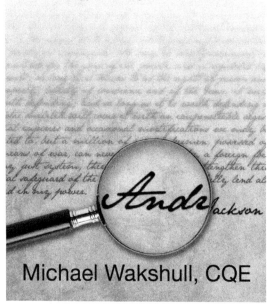

Line by Line

Forensic Document Examination
A Strategy for Legal Professionals

Michael Wakshull, CQE

Other Books by Michael Wakshull

Line By Line – Forensic Document Examination – A
Strategy for Legal Professionals

ISBN: 978-0-9857294-0-0

Also available for Amazon Kindle:
http://amzn.com/B00CB7MFXU

About The Author

Michael Wakshull, president of Q9 Consulting, is a civil and criminal court-qualified forensic document examiner based in Temecula, California. Services provided to clients throughout the U.S. include authentication of handwritten and computer-generated documents. Using a science-based approach, he partners with legal clients to dissect the evidence presented in documents.

Wakshull holds a Master of Science Degree in technology management from the University of Denver and a graduate school certificate in forensic document examination from the Department of Criminal Justice and Criminology at East Tennessee State University.

He has spoken at several international forensic conferences including the World Congress of Forensics in China. He authors and presents document examination courses for minimum continuing legal education (MCLE). Wakshull applies his technology skills, acquired while managing and implementing global information systems and quality systems projects, to forensic document examination.
A National Speakers Association member, he is available to speak on these subjects.

Wakshull is a member of the National Association of Document Examiners (NADE), acting president of the San Diego Chapter of Forensic Expert Witness Association (FEWA), and a member of ASTM International. In 2012 Wakshull was chair of the NADE conference in San Diego, CA. He is an adjunct instructor at Bellevue University and University of Redlands.